A No-BS Guide to M
for Your Vision

SECTION 1: WHY YOU'RE HERE (AND WHAT'S POSSIBLE NOW)

The Creative Revolution Is Happening (And It's Here to Help)

We're in the middle of the most significant creative transformation since the internet itself. The digital content creation market has grown to nearly $80 billion in 2025, opening doors that were previously closed to most of us. If you've been feeling overwhelmed by all the skills needed to bring your ideas to life, you're not alone—and there's good news on the horizon.

The truth is, we all face barriers when trying to create: technical limitations, time constraints, budget restrictions, or simply not knowing where to start. It's frustrating when you have a clear vision in your mind but lack the tools or skills to make it real. That gap between imagination and execution has stopped countless brilliant ideas from ever seeing the light of day.

But here's the heartening truth: you don't need to be a tech wizard to thrive in this new creative landscape.

This isn't about machines replacing human creativity—quite the opposite. It's about AI handling the technical hurdles and repetitive tasks that have been holding you back, freeing you to focus on what humans do brilliantly: having original ideas, understanding emotional nuance, and bringing your unique perspective that no algorithm could ever replicate.

The distance between dreaming something up and making it happen has never been smaller. Projects that once required teams of specialists and months of work can now be accomplished by one person in days or even hours. This is what we mean by the democratization of creativity—the tools of production are becoming accessible to everyone, not just those with specialized training or substantial resources.

What AI Actually Is (And How It Fits Into Your Creative Process)

Let's demystify AI, because understanding this technology is the first step to making it work for you rather than feeling intimidated by it.

At its heart, AI is pattern recognition on a massive scale. These systems have been trained on enormous amounts of data—text, images, code, audio—and have learned to recognize patterns and generate new content based on those patterns. When you interact with AI, you're essentially giving it direction about what patterns to create or continue based on your needs.

What AI is NOT:

- It's not conscious or sentient
- It's not a replacement for your creative vision
- It's not perfect or immune to mistakes

- It's not able to understand your intentions without clear guidance

What AI IS:

- It's an amplifier for your ideas and capabilities
- It's a tireless assistant that can handle repetitive tasks
- It's a bridge across technical gaps in your skillset
- It's a collaborator that can suggest unexpected connections and possibilities

Think of AI as a particularly talented assistant: eager to help, technically proficient, but completely dependent on your guidance and direction. Without your vision steering the process, even the most advanced AI is just generating random variations with no purpose or soul.

The beauty of modern AI tools is that they meet you where you are. Struggling with writer's block? AI can help generate initial ideas or flesh out your outline. Not a designer but need visual elements? AI can create images based on your descriptions. Overwhelmed by technical barriers? AI can handle the complex parts while you focus on the creative direction.

The goal isn't to hand over your creative process—it's to remove the obstacles that have been holding your creativity hostage.

The CEO Mindset

The most common mistake people make is approaching AI as passive users rather than active directors.

A user says: "Make me a logo." A CEO says: "Create a minimalist logo that reflects themes of growth and sustainability, using shades of green and blue, suitable for a tech startup in the environmental space."

See the difference? The user leaves all the important decisions to the AI, which often leads to generic results. The CEO provides clear direction while still giving the AI room to do what it does best—executing on a well-defined vision.

You don't need to understand the technical complexities of neural networks or transformer models. What you do need to understand is how to lead the creative process:

1. How to communicate your vision clearly and specifically
2. How to evaluate outputs constructively and identify what's working versus what needs improvement
3. How to guide the process through thoughtful iteration
4. How to recognize when AI is the right tool versus when human expertise would be more valuable

Your true advantage isn't technical knowledge—it's your creative vision, your taste, and your ability to direct these powerful tools toward your specific goals. In the AI era, the people who thrive aren't necessarily those who understand the technology best, but those who know most clearly what they want to create and can guide the tools accordingly.

This approach transforms AI from something potentially intimidating into something empowering. Instead of feeling like you need to keep up with every technical advancement, you can focus on developing the visionary and directorial skills that no AI possesses.

Remember that even the most advanced AI tools are instruments waiting to be played. They don't make music on their own—they need a conductor. That's you.

SECTION 2: DEFINE THE VISION (THINK LIKE A CREATIVE DIRECTOR)

Dreaming Without Limits

The first step to becoming the CEO of your imagination is recognizing and gently dismantling the self-imposed limitations that have been holding your creativity captive.

Before AI, your creative ambitions were likely constrained by very real barriers:

- Technical skills you never had the opportunity to develop
- Budget limitations that kept professional help out of reach
- Time constraints that made ambitious projects impractical
- Limited access to specialized talent and expertise

These constraints haven't disappeared completely, but they've been dramatically reduced. The question is shifting from "Can I possibly do this?" to "How can I best define what I want to create?"

This is your permission to dream bigger than you've allowed yourself before. Have you wanted to write a book but struggled with structuring long-form content? Create a podcast but were intimidated by audio production? Launch a brand but lacked design skills? Develop a product but didn't know where to start? Build an online course but felt overwhelmed by the technical aspects?

All of these projects are now within reach as primarily solo endeavors, with AI tools handling many of the technical and production elements that previously required specialized skills or teams.

But with this expanded possibility comes a new challenge: when more is possible, how do you decide what to focus on?

Start by asking yourself these questions:

- What creative projects have I abandoned or never started because the technical barriers seemed too high?
- What unique perspective or value can I offer that others don't?
- What would I create if skills and technical limitations weren't factors in the equation?

At this early stage, resist the urge to edit or critique your ideas. There will be plenty of time for practical considerations later. For now, give yourself the gift of unbounded imagination.

Sketching Your Vision

Now that you've given yourself permission to dream bigger, it's time to get specific about what you're creating. This is where you translate your expansive ideas into something concrete and actionable.

Great creative directors don't just operate on vague notions—they create comprehensive briefs that serve as roadmaps. This becomes even more important when working with AI, which thrives on clear direction but can flounder with ambiguity.

Start by creating a vision board—digital or physical—that captures the aesthetic, tone, and key elements of what you're trying to create. This becomes a visual reference point you can return to whenever you feel lost in the details or whenever you need to reconnect with your original inspiration.

Next, write a creative brief for yourself that answers these key questions:

- What exactly am I creating? (Be specific: "A 10-episode podcast about sustainable investing for millennials" is much clearer than "A podcast about money")
- Who is it for? (Describe your ideal audience with enough detail that you could recognize them)
- What problem does it solve or need does it fulfill?
- What emotional response do you want to evoke?
- What practical outcome do you want for your audience?
- What's the style, tone, and aesthetic that aligns with your vision?
- What similar successful examples can you reference for inspiration?

This brief becomes your North Star—the standard against which you'll measure every AI output. When you're uncertain about whether something is working, return to this document and ask, "Does this serve the vision I've defined?"

Having this clarity doesn't restrict creativity—it actually enables it by providing boundaries within which you can explore deeply rather than wandering aimlessly. AI tools work best when given clear parameters and direction, making your vision document not just helpful but essential to the process.

's success wasn't just using AI tools—it was having a crystal-clear vision of what she wanted to create and directing the tools accordingly.

Finding Your Creative Advantage

Your unique advantage in an AI-powered world comes from the combination of:

- Your specific knowledge and expertise
- Your personal taste and aesthetic sensibilities
- Your understanding of your audience
- Your ability to direct and curate AI outputs

AI excels at execution but struggles with originality and purpose. It can help you realize your vision but can't provide the vision itself. This is where your human capabilities shine brightest.

Many people worry about AI making their skills obsolete, but the reality is more nuanced. AI tools are removing technical barriers that have prevented people from expressing their creativity, not replacing the need for creative direction.

Start by identifying the aspects of your creative process that are uniquely human:

- Personal experiences that inform your perspective
- Specialized knowledge in your field
- Cultural understanding and contextual awareness
- Emotional intelligence and empathy for your audience
- Taste and discernment about what works

These become your creative advantage—the elements that no AI can replicate and that differentiate your work from others who might be using the same tools.

Think about areas where you've struggled with execution in the past. Maybe you have brilliant ideas but struggle with writing fluently, or perhaps you can envision beautiful designs but lack the technical skills to create them. AI can help bridge these gaps, allowing your vision to shine through without being limited by technical constraints.

Remember: in a world where execution is increasingly automated, vision, taste, and creative direction become the ultimate competitive advantages. The question isn't whether AI can do what you do—it's whether you can direct AI to help you express your unique creative perspective more fully than was previously possible.

SECTION 3: DIRECT THE MACHINE (PROMPT LIKE A PRO, NOT A ROBOT)

The Art of Prompting

If you're going to be the CEO of your imagination, you need to master the primary way you'll communicate with your AI collaborators: the prompt.

A prompt isn't just a request—it's a form of creative direction that guides the AI toward your vision. The difference between mediocre and exceptional results often comes down to how well you can communicate what you want.

Think of prompting as learning a new language—one that bridges your creative vision and the AI's capabilities. Like any language, it takes a little practice, but you'll improve quickly, and the results are worth the effort.

The anatomy of an effective prompt consists of three key elements:

1. **Clarity**: Specific, unambiguous instructions about what you want to create.
2. **Context**: Background information that helps the AI understand the bigger picture of your project.
3. **Constraints**: Boundaries and guidelines that keep the output aligned with your vision.

Here's what this looks like in practice:

Basic prompt: "Write me a blog post about sustainability."

Effective prompt: "Write a 1,200-word blog post about practical sustainability initiatives for small e-commerce businesses with limited budgets. The tone should be practical and solution-oriented, focusing on cost-saving opportunities. Include 5 specific actions readers can implement immediately, and format with clear headings, bullet points, and a concluding call to action."

The difference is striking. The basic prompt leaves everything to interpretation, while the effective prompt provides clear parameters that guide the AI toward a specific, useful outcome.

Common prompting challenges you might encounter:

- Being too vague or general about what you want
- Forgetting to include important context about purpose or audience
- Not specifying tone or style elements
- Omitting formatting instructions
- Trying to get too many different things in a single prompt

These issues are completely normal when you're starting out. Think of early prompting attempts as drafts—each iteration gets you closer to mastery.

Your Prompting Toolkit

Certain prompt structures and phrases consistently deliver better results across AI tools. Think of these as your creative direction templates—ready to adapt for any project.

For Brainstorming and Ideation:

Generate 10 unique ideas for [specific purpose] targeted at [specific audience].

Each idea should:

- Address the challenge of [problem statement]
- Be achievable with [available resources]
- Have a distinct advantage or approach

Format as a numbered list with a clear title and 2-3 sentence description for each idea.

This structure works well because it gives the AI enough constraints to generate focused ideas while still allowing room for creativity within those boundaries.

For Content Creation:

Write a [content type] about [specific topic] for [specific audience].

Tone: [descriptive adjectives for tone]

Length: [word count or parameters]

Structure: [outline or formatting requirements]

Key points to include:

- [Point 1]
- [Point 2]
- [Point 3]

Include a compelling [call to action/conclusion/introduction] that emphasizes [key benefit or takeaway].

When you provide this level of detail, you're much more likely to get content that aligns with your vision from the first draft.

For Visual Design Direction:

Create a [type of visual] that depicts [subject matter].

Style: [reference artists, movements, or aesthetic]

Mood: [emotional qualities]

Colors: [color palette or scheme]

Composition: [layout directions]

Important elements to include: [must-have components]

Elements to avoid: [what doesn't belong]
Visual AI tools respond remarkably well to specific references and emotional direction. Don't be afraid to name specific artists or styles that inspire you.

For Strategic Planning:

Develop a [timeframe] plan for [specific goal].

Context: [relevant background information]

Available resources: [what you have to work with]

Constraints: [limitations to consider]

Key milestones should include:

- [Milestone 1]

- [Milestone 2]

- [Milestone 3]

Format as a week-by-week timeline with specific actions and outcomes for each period.

This approach helps transform big-picture goals into actionable steps—something AI excels at when given proper context.

The Progressive Prompting Approach

For complex projects, use a "progressive prompting" approach—a conversation rather than a single request:

1. **Start with a foundation**: Begin with a general direction to establish the basic framework
2. **Provide feedback**: Respond with specific guidance about what's working and what needs adjustment
3. **Refine with details**: Focus on particular elements that need improvement
4. **Finalize with precision**: Make targeted adjustments to perfect the result

This iterative approach often produces better results than trying to get everything perfect in a single prompt. It also more closely resembles how you'd work with a human creative partner.

Remember that prompting is a skill that improves with practice. Keep track of prompts that work well for you and build your own library of effective direction styles. The more you work with AI tools, the more intuitive this process will become.

Voice, Character, and Style Direction

One of the most powerful ways to use AI is to have it adapt to your unique voice or create content in a specific style. This requires clear direction about the characteristics you want in the communication.

Many creators struggle with maintaining a consistent voice across all their content—it's one of the most common creative roadblocks. AI can help overcome this challenge when you provide the right guidance.

To establish a consistent voice or style:

1. **Create a simple style guide** for your AI that defines:
   - Vocabulary preferences (formal vs. casual, technical vs. accessible)
   - Sentence structure tendencies (short and punchy vs. flowing and descriptive)
   - Metaphors or analogies that resonate with your audience
   - Phrases you commonly use or intentionally avoid
   - Humor style (if appropriate)
   - Values that should shine through in the content
2. **Provide concrete examples** of the style you want to emulate: "Write in the style of the following example: [insert paragraph that exemplifies your desired style]" This approach is often more effective than trying to describe a style in abstract terms. The AI can analyze the example and extract patterns much as it would learn from any other source.
3. **Use character or personality references** to shorthand complicated style directions: "Write

this as if you were Anthony Bourdain explaining complex concepts with straightforward language, colorful metaphors, and a touch of irreverent humor." This works surprisingly well because these personalities have distinctive communication styles that the AI has encountered in its training.

4. **Create a consistent "voice reminder"** that you can include at the beginning of prompts for ongoing projects: "Remember to maintain our brand voice: confident but not arrogant, technical but accessible, and always focused on practical benefits rather than hype."

By being intentional about voice and style direction, you can achieve a consistency across your AI-assisted content that might have been difficult to maintain on your own, especially when creating content at scale or when you're feeling creatively drained.

The goal isn't to replace your voice, but to help you maintain it consistently across all your creative outputs, even when you're stretched thin or working on multiple projects simultaneously.

Real-World Examples That Work

Let's look at some prompt templates for common creative projects that you can adapt for your own needs. These are battle-tested approaches that consistently produce useful results.

Book Outline Development

If you've ever wanted to write a book but felt overwhelmed by the structure, this prompt can help:

Create a detailed outline for a non-fiction book titled "[Title]" about [subject].

Target audience: [reader description]
Book's primary promise: [what readers will gain]

The book should have 3 parts with 3-4 chapters each. For each chapter, provide:
- A compelling chapter title
- 3-5 bullet points covering key concepts
- A brief description of how this chapter serves the overall narrative

The tone should be [tone description], and the writing style should be similar to authors like [reference authors].
This approach breaks down the intimidating task of book planning into manageable components while ensuring the structure serves your overall vision.

Brand Messaging Framework

For entrepreneurs struggling to articulate their brand identity consistently:

Develop a brand messaging framework for [company/product], a [brief description].

Include:
1. Mission statement (one sentence)
2. Vision statement (one sentence)
3. Value proposition (1-2 sentences)
4. Brand personality (3-5 adjectives with brief explanations)
5. Core messaging pillars (3-4 key themes with supporting points)
6. Tagline options (5 variations)
7. Brand voice characteristics (how the brand speaks)

Our target audience is [audience description], and our primary competitors are [competitor list].
This structure helps create consistency across all your brand communications—something that often requires expensive agency support.

Social Media Content Calendar

For content creators who struggle with consistency and planning:

Create a 2-week social media content plan for [brand] focused on [theme/campaign].

For each day, provide:
1. The platform (Instagram, Twitter, LinkedIn, etc.)
2. Content type (image, carousel, video, poll, etc.)
3. Draft copy (including hashtags where relevant)

4. Content purpose (educate, engage, entertain, or convert)
5. A brief description of the visual element

Our brand voice is [voice description], and we want to emphasize [key messages].
Ensure variety in post formats and purposes while maintaining a cohesive theme.
This approach transforms the overwhelming task of social media planning into a structured process that you can repeat and refine.

Design Brief

For projects where you can visualize what you want but struggle to create it:

Create a design brief for a [design project type] for [company/product].

Project overview: [brief description of the project]
Brand background: [relevant brand information]
Design objectives: [what the design needs to accomplish]
Target audience: [who will engage with the design]
Key messages: [what the design should communicate]
Visual style: [aesthetic direction, including reference examples if possible]

Deliverables needed: [specific formats, sizes, variations]

Timeline: [key milestones and deadlines]

Include any specific elements that must be incorporated and any design approaches to avoid.

A well-crafted design brief bridges the gap between your vision and what an AI image generator can produce.

These templates aren't rigid formulas but starting points you can customize. The structure they provide helps overcome the common creative block of staring at a blank page, unsure where to begin. They're especially valuable when you're tackling a creative project type for the first time or when you're feeling creatively drained but still need to produce high-quality work.

SECTION 4: BUILD IT OUT (EXECUTION IS QUEEN)

The Tool Ecosystem (2025 Edition)

The AI tool landscape continues to evolve rapidly, but it can be overwhelming to figure out which tools are worth your time and which are just hype. Here's your curated guide to the most effective tools for creative work in 2025, organized by purpose:

Text Generation and Writing

1. **Claude by Anthropic** - Excels at long-form content, nuanced writing, and maintaining consistent tone. Perfect for books, articles, and in-depth creative writing when you need a thoughtful, human-like approach.
2. **ChatGPT (GPT-4)** - Versatile and widely accessible. Particularly strong at technical writing, code generation, and structured content. Great for projects requiring both writing and technical elements.
3. **Perplexity** - Research-focused AI that provides citations and comprehensive analysis. Ideal when you need fact-checking and information gathering as part of your creative process.
4. **Writesonic** - Specialized for marketing copy and conversion-focused content. Includes templates for ads, emails, and landing pages that help overcome the "blank page" problem in marketing.
5. **Type.ai** - A dedicated AI writing platform that combines word processing with AI assistance. Great for longer projects requiring consistency throughout multiple sessions.

Image Creation

1. **Leonardo.ai** - Offers multiple models including the powerful Phoenix model. Excellent for photorealistic imagery and consistent character generation across multiple images.
2. **Midjourney** - Outstanding for artistic and creative imagery with a distinctive style. Best for conceptual illustrations and artistic projects where you need visual impact.
3. **Adobe Firefly** - Integrated with Creative Cloud apps and focused on commercial-safe content

generation. Ideal for professional design work within established workflows.

4. **Canva with Magic Design** - The easiest entry point for non-designers, with templates and user-friendly AI design tools that help bridge the technical gap in visual creation.

5. **Lummi** - Specialized in unique, high-quality image generation for web design and marketing materials with professionally usable results.

Audio and Video

1. **Murf.ai** - Creates realistic voiceovers in multiple languages. Perfect for narration, presentations, and educational content when recording yourself isn't practical.

2. **Synthesia** - Produces AI video presenter content. Great for training videos, product demos, and simple explainer content without needing a recording studio.

3. **Pika** - Generates short video clips from text prompts. Useful for social media content and B-roll footage to enhance your productions.

4. **NotebookLM** - Google's tool that generates podcast-style conversations from written content. Excellent for creating dialogue-based audio from your existing materials.

5. **Descript** - Audio and video editing with AI transcription and voice cloning features. Ideal for podcast production and video editing when you need to make changes to recorded content.

Project Organization

1. **Notion AI** - Note-taking and project management with integrated AI assistance.

Great for planning and organizing complex creative projects from inception to completion.

2. **Airtable with AI Fields** - Database and project management with AI capabilities for content generation and data analysis. Perfect for managing content calendars and production schedules.

3. **HubSpot AI Tools** - Marketing automation with AI content generation. Perfect for campaign management and customer communications when you need to maintain consistency at scale.

Choosing the Right Tool for the Job

When selecting tools for your creative stack, consider these factors:

1. **Purpose fit**: Does the tool specialize in the type of content you're creating? A specialized tool often produces better results than a general one.

2. **Integration**: Does it work well with your other tools and platforms? Smooth workflows between tools save tremendous time and frustration.

3. **Output quality**: Does it consistently produce results that match your standards? Test each tool with your specific use cases before committing.

4. **Learning curve**: How quickly can you become proficient with it? Consider whether the time investment to master a complex tool is worth it for your specific needs.

5. **Budget**: Is the subscription cost justified by the value it provides? Sometimes paying for the right tool saves money in the long run by improving your productivity.

Start with a small core of tools rather than trying to use everything at once. A focused toolkit that you master will serve you better than dozens of tools you barely understand. You can always expand your toolkit as your needs evolve.

From Drafts to Deliverables

Creating with AI is an iterative process, not a one-and-done magic trick. Here's a framework for moving efficiently from your initial concept to a polished final product:

The Four-Stage Creative Workflow

1. **Generation** (10-20% of your time)
   - Use AI to produce multiple versions or approaches
   - Focus on quantity over quality at this stage
   - Experiment with different prompts and directions
   - Don't get attached to any single output yet
2. **Curation** (10% of your time)
   - Select the most promising outputs that align with your vision
   - Identify specific strengths and weaknesses in each
   - Make high-level decisions about direction
   - Trust your instincts about what feels right
3. **Refinement** (50-60% of your time)

- Direct AI to improve specific aspects of chosen outputs
- Combine elements from different versions
- Add your unique human touch and expertise
- Iterate until the quality meets your standards
- This is where most of the real work happens

4. **Finalization** (20% of your time)

- Make final edits and adjustments
- Format for the intended platform or medium
- Review for consistency with your overall vision
- Prepare for distribution or implementation
- Don't rush this stage—details matter

This workflow applies whether you're writing a book, designing a brand identity, or creating a content marketing campaign. The proportions might shift depending on your project, but the basic structure remains effective.

A common mistake is expecting perfection from the initial generation phase. Remember that AI tools are collaborators, not mind readers. The first outputs are starting points, not finished products. The magic happens in the refinement phase, where your creative direction shapes the raw material into something truly aligned with your vision.

The Feedback Loop

Effective refinement relies on giving clear, specific feedback when an AI output isn't quite right. Avoid vague instructions like "make it better" or "this doesn't work." Instead, provide actionable direction:

- "The tone is too formal. Rewrite using more conversational language and shorter sentences."
- "The concept is good but the visual style doesn't match our brand. Revise using our color palette of deep blues and teals, with more minimalist composition."
- "The structure works but the examples aren't relevant to our audience. Replace them with scenarios focused on small business challenges."

Think of feedback as gentle course correction rather than starting over. Each iteration should move you closer to your vision. If you find yourself going in circles, step back and reassess whether your initial vision was clear enough or if you've chosen the right tool for the job.

This approach transforms the often frustrating experience of trying to get an AI to "understand" what you want into a collaborative process where each step builds on the last.

Building in Public vs. Building in Private

There are two schools of thought on sharing AI-assisted creative work:

Building in public advantages:

- Real-time feedback from your audience
- Building anticipation for the final product

- Demonstrating your process and expertise
- Creating content about your creation process

Building in private advantages:

- Freedom to experiment without judgment
- No pressure to explain your process
- Ability to control the narrative around your work
- Surprise factor when you launch the finished product

The right approach depends on your personality, audience, and the nature of your project. Many successful creators opt for a hybrid approach: building the foundation in private, then sharing selected aspects of the process once the direction is solidified.

Tracking Progress

Keep a creative dashboard that tracks:

- Key milestones achieved
- Current focus areas
- Open questions or challenges
- Next actions
- Target completion dates

This gives you a bird's-eye view of your project and helps prevent getting lost in the details. It also provides motivation as you see your progress over time.

Integration Strategies

Creating content with AI is just the beginning. The real value comes from integrating that content into your broader creative ecosystem.

Building a Content Engine

Instead of producing isolated pieces of content, think in terms of building a content engine that can consistently generate material for multiple platforms and purposes.

Start by creating cornerstone content—substantial, high-value material like guides, videos, or courses. Then use AI to help you:

1. **Extract**: Pull key ideas, quotes, and insights from your cornerstone content
2. **Transform**: Convert these elements into different formats (text to image, long-form to short-form)
3. **Distribute**: Adapt the content for different platforms while maintaining a consistent message
4. **Connect**: Create pathways that lead audiences from bite-sized content back to your cornerstone material

This approach maximizes the value of your creative work while maintaining coherence across your entire content ecosystem.

Automation Opportunities

Look for repetitive aspects of your creative process that can be automated to free up your mental energy for the truly creative work only you can do:

- **Content curation**: Use AI to gather relevant articles, trends, and discussion topics in your field
- **Initial drafts and outlines**: Start with AI-generated structures that you can refine

- **Social media posting**: Schedule and distribute content across platforms
- **Email newsletter formatting**: Maintain consistent layouts and sections
- **Basic image editing**: Resize, crop, and optimize images for different platforms
- **Transcription and summarization**: Convert audio or video to text, or long text to key points
- **Data analysis**: Extract insights from performance metrics and audience feedback

By identifying and automating these routine tasks, you preserve your creative energy for the aspects of creation that require human judgment and expertise. This isn't about cutting corners—it's about strategic allocation of your most precious resource: your attention and creative energy.

Many creators feel guilty about automating parts of their process, as if it somehow makes their work less authentic. But think of it this way: a novelist doesn't handcraft their own paper before writing, and a painter doesn't need to create their own pigments from scratch. Using tools to handle the mechanical aspects allows you to focus on the creative essence of your work.

Template Development

As you refine your creative process, develop templates for recurring tasks:

- **Prompt templates**: Pre-built structures for generating different types of content
- **Design frameworks**: Basic layouts and elements that maintain visual consistency
- **Content structures**: Repeatable formats that you can adapt and populate

- **Workflow checklists**: Process guides to ensure quality and completeness

These templates become valuable intellectual property that speeds up your process and ensures consistency across your work. They're particularly useful when:

- You're working on multiple projects simultaneously
- You need to delegate parts of the process to collaborators
- You're creating series or collections that should have a unified feel
- You find yourself solving the same problems repeatedly

Start simple and refine your templates based on what works. Over time, you'll build a personal creative system that combines the efficiency of automation with your unique vision and expertise.

Mini Case Study: 30-Day Launch

Alex was an investment advisor who wanted to launch a niche newsletter about sustainable investing—a subject they were passionate about but had struggled to find time to develop alongside their full-time work. Here's how they used AI to go from concept to launch in 30 days:

Days 1-3: Vision and Strategy

- Created a detailed creative brief defining the newsletter's purpose, audience, and unique angle
- Used Claude to develop a content strategy and editorial calendar, focusing on topics they had expertise in

- Designed a simple brand identity using Midjourney and Canva that conveyed professionalism with a modern edge

Days 4-10: Foundation Building

- Built a landing page with AI-generated copy that clearly communicated the newsletter's value proposition
- Created a lead magnet (a beginner's guide to sustainable investing) with Claude and Canva
- Set up automation for email delivery and social posting to minimize ongoing administrative work
- Developed templates for recurring newsletter sections to ensure consistency and save time

Days 11-20: Content Creation

- Wrote the first four newsletter issues with Claude, using their industry knowledge to guide and refine the AI's output
- Created supporting social media content with ChatGPT that would drive traffic to the newsletter
- Generated custom graphics for each issue with Midjourney to make the content more engaging
- Recorded audio versions of each newsletter with Murf to offer flexibility for subscribers

Days 21-25: Testing and Refinement

- Tested all automated systems to ensure a smooth subscriber experience
- Shared with a small beta group of colleagues for feedback, making key adjustments
- Refined content templates and brand voice based on what resonated most with test readers

- Adjusted the strategy to emphasize the topics that generated the most interest

Days 26-30: Launch and Promotion

- Published the landing page and lead magnet
- Executed a social media launch campaign targeting relevant communities
- Released the first official newsletter issue to build momentum
- Engaged with initial subscriber comments and questions to build community

The result: Alex launched a fully-formed newsletter with four issues ready to go, complete with audio versions and supporting social content. Without AI, this would have taken months of work or required a team of freelancers.

The key success factors were:

1. Starting with a clear vision that leveraged Alex's existing expertise
2. Creating templates and systems that ensured consistency and efficiency
3. Using the right AI tools for each specific task
4. Maintaining human curation and direction throughout the process
5. Building in time for testing and refinement before the public launch

This approach allowed Alex to overcome the time constraints that had previously prevented them from sharing their knowledge. The newsletter quickly gained traction in the sustainable investing community and eventually became a significant additional income stream.

SECTION 5: STAY THE CEO (CREATIVE AUTHORITY & KEEPING THE VIBE)

Maintaining Creative Authority

As AI tools become more powerful, there's a real risk of letting them lead rather than follow. Here's how to stay firmly in control of your creative process:

Developing Your Creative Judgment

Your taste—your ability to distinguish between good and great, between generic and distinctive—is something no AI possesses. Think of it as your creative superpower in an increasingly AI-assisted world.

To strengthen this essential muscle:

1. **Study the masters in your field** to understand what excellence truly looks like. Analyze why certain work endures while other pieces feel dated or forgettable.
2. **Articulate why** certain creative works resonate with you and others don't. Being able to verbalize these judgments helps refine your taste.
3. **Compare different versions** of AI outputs to identify what specifically works better and why. This practice trains your eye to notice subtleties.
4. **Seek feedback from people** whose taste you respect, especially those who might see things differently than you do.

5. **Regularly review your own work** critically, identifying what you'd improve if you were starting over. This builds self-awareness about your creative evolution.

This discernment is what separates people who merely use AI tools from those who direct them toward truly distinctive creative outcomes.

When to Trust Your Judgment Over AI Suggestions

Learn to recognize situations where your judgment should override the AI:

- When the AI suggests "safe" options that lack originality or personality
- When recommendations conflict with your brand values or voice
- When the output feels generic rather than distinctive to your vision
- When the AI misunderstands cultural context or nuance
- When your intuition strongly suggests a different approach

Remember that AI is trained on existing work, which can lead to regression toward the mean—the average of what's already been done. Your job is to push beyond the predictable toward the exceptional and distinctive.

It's normal to sometimes doubt your judgment, especially when an AI tool confidently presents something that doesn't feel right. But that very hesitation is often your creative intuition trying to tell you something important. Listen to it.

Building a Unique Creative Perspective

To avoid creating AI-generic content that could have been made by anyone, focus on developing what only you can bring:

1. **Develop strong points of view** that inform your creative choices. Neutrality rarely creates memorable work—having a perspective does.
2. **Incorporate your unique experiences and insights** that AI can't replicate. Your personal and professional journey contains wisdom that no model has been trained on.
3. **Create unusual combinations of influences and references** from different domains. Cross-pollination between fields often leads to the most innovative work.
4. **Question conventional wisdom** in your field. The most interesting creative work often comes from asking "why do we always do it this way?"
5. **Use AI outputs as starting points**, not final products. Think of them as clay to be shaped by your vision, not sculptures to be displayed as-is.

The most successful creators in the AI age aren't those who use AI most skillfully, but those who bring the strongest human perspective to their work. They understand that technological tools are the means, not the end.

Many creators worry about their work becoming indistinguishable from AI-generated content. The antidote is leaning into the aspects of your creativity that are distinctly yours—your experiences, your quirks, your obsessions, your unique way of seeing the world.

Protecting Your Voice and Values

As you integrate AI into your creative process, be mindful of maintaining authenticity and alignment with your values.

Ensuring Ethical Use

Set personal guidelines for your AI use that address:

- How transparent you want to be about AI involvement in your work
- Your boundaries around intellectual property and creative attribution
- Avoiding misrepresentation or deception with AI-generated content
- Considering the social impact of what you create
- Maintaining human oversight of important decisions

These guidelines will evolve as technology and cultural norms change, but having explicit principles helps you navigate gray areas confidently.

Many creators worry about whether using AI is "cheating" or somehow diminishes the value of their work. Remember that all creative tools—from word processors to cameras to design software—were once new technologies that raised similar questions. What matters is not the tools you use but how you use them and to what end.

Maintaining Authenticity

Authenticity doesn't mean avoiding AI—it means using AI in service of your genuine creative vision rather than letting it replace your voice.

Practices that support authenticity:

1. **Start with your ideas and vision**, then use AI to develop them—not the reverse. Your original concept should always drive the process.
2. **Edit AI outputs** to align with your natural voice and perspective. Never accept first drafts without your personal touch.
3. **Add personal anecdotes and experiences** that are uniquely yours. These connections to your life and work cannot be replicated.
4. **Inject your specific knowledge** that the AI doesn't have—your professional expertise, cultural insights, or specialized understanding.
5. **Trust your instincts** when something doesn't feel authentic to you, even if you can't immediately articulate why.

Many creators find that AI actually helps them sound more like themselves, not less. By handling technical aspects they find challenging, AI can remove barriers that previously prevented their authentic voice from shining through.

Disclosure Practices

Norms around disclosing AI use are still evolving, but transparency builds trust. Consider:

- When disclosure serves your audience (educational content, professional contexts)
- How disclosure affects perception of your work
- Industry standards and expectations in your field
- Your personal comfort level with transparency

There's no one-size-fits-all approach here. A photographer might disclose AI-enhanced editing on commercial work but not on personal artistic projects.

A writer might mention AI assistance in research but not in drafting. A designer might be open about using AI for initial concepts but emphasize the human refinement process.

What matters is making intentional choices rather than defaulting to either complete secrecy or unnecessary over-disclosure. Ask yourself: what would my audience want to know, and what aligns with my values?

Sustainable Creative Leadership

The abundance of AI tools can lead to a paradoxical outcome: creative burnout amidst unprecedented resources. Here's how to maintain a sustainable creative practice:

Avoiding AI Burnout and Dependency

1. **Set boundaries around tool use**. Designate specific days or times for AI experimentation versus focused, non-assisted work.
2. **Practice analog creation regularly**. Maintain skills and perspectives that don't rely on digital tools or electricity.
3. **Distinguish between creation and consumption**. Using AI tools can sometimes feel productive when you're actually just consuming outputs without advancing your vision.
4. **Monitor how different tools affect your energy**. Some AI interactions may energize you while others deplete you—adjust accordingly.

Tool Quick-Start Guides

Essential Settings and Configurations

For Claude:

- Use the "temperature" setting to control creativity vs. consistency (lower = more consistent, higher = more creative)
- For longer projects, use Claude's "memory" feature to maintain context across sessions
- Save successful prompts in a personal library for reuse
- Try both chat and document mode depending on your project needs

For Midjourney:

- Start with "/describe" on a reference image to learn effective prompt language
- Use the "stylize" parameter (1-1000) to control how artistic vs. literal the results are
- Add "--no" parameters to exclude unwanted elements
- Use version 6 for photorealism, version 5.2 for more artistic interpretations

For Leonardo.ai:

- Begin with the Phoenix model for general purposes
- Experiment with LoRA models for consistent character generation
- Save successful prompts and generations to your collection for reuse
- Use the negative prompt feature to refine results

For Murf.ai:

- Upload your script as a text file for easier editing

- Use punctuation to control pacing (commas for short pauses, periods for longer ones)
- Add [pause:2s] tags to create natural breaks
- Adjust speed settings to 90-95% for more natural delivery

Free Trial Information

Most AI tools offer generous free tiers or trial periods that let you experiment before committing:

- **Claude**: Free tier with limitations, affordable monthly subscription for full features
- **ChatGPT**: Robust free version, premium tier for GPT-4 access and priority during peak times
- **Midjourney**: Trial credits for new users, subscription tiers based on usage needs
- **Leonardo.ai**: Free tier with daily generation credits, premium plans for higher volume
- **Murf.ai**: Free plan with limited minutes, affordable monthly plans for regular users
- **Canva**: Extensive free tier, premium features available on paid plans

Don't feel pressured to subscribe to everything at once. Start with the free tiers to identify which tools align best with your creative process, then invest in the ones that deliver the most value.

Community Connections

The fastest way to master these tools is to learn from others using them creatively:

- **Discord communities**: Many AI tools have official Discord servers with dedicated channels for sharing work, techniques, and troubleshooting

- **Reddit**: Communities like r/ArtificialInteligence, r/midjourney, and r/ChatGPT share latest developments and creative uses
- **Twitter/X**: Follow hashtags like #AIart, #AIwriting, and #PromptEngineering to see cutting-edge applications
- **YouTube tutorials**: Channels dedicated to specific tools often reveal techniques that aren't documented in official guides

Remember that the community around these tools is often as valuable as the tools themselves. Many creators are generous with their knowledge and willing to help newcomers navigate the learning curve.

Vision Check-In Worksheet

Use this simple framework periodically to assess your creative direction and relationship with AI tools:

Alignment Check

- Is my current work aligned with my original vision?
- Are the AI tools enhancing or distracting from my core creative goals?
- What aspects of my original vision am I executing well, and what areas need attention?

Progress Tracking

- What have I completed in the last week/month that moves me closer to my vision?
- Which tools or approaches have been most effective?

- What unexpected challenges or opportunities have emerged?

Inspiration Renewal

- What recently inspired me that I could incorporate into my work?
- Which creative voices or examples am I learning from right now?
- What experiment could I try that might lead to a breakthrough?

Next-Level Challenges

- What's one area where I could push my current work further?
- Is there a skill I need to develop to better direct the AI tools?
- What would make my work stand out more distinctly from generic AI outputs?

Take 15-20 minutes with these questions whenever you feel stuck or uncertain about your direction. They help reconnect you with your original purpose while adapting to what you've learned along the way.###

Building in Public vs. Building in Private

There are two approaches to sharing AI-assisted creative work, and each has its merits depending on your personality and goals:

Building in public advantages:

- Receive real-time feedback that can improve your work
- Create anticipation and interest before your final launch
- Demonstrate your process and expertise to potential clients or customers

- Generate additional content by documenting your creation journey
- Build community around your work as it develops

For many creators, showing the messy middle of the process can be intimidating. We naturally want to present only our polished, finished work. But there's something powerful about letting others see how your vision evolves—it makes your creative process more approachable and often builds stronger connections with your audience.

Building in private advantages:

- Work without external pressure or premature judgment
- Avoid the need to explain your process or defend works-in-progress
- Maintain control over how your work is perceived
- Preserve the impact of a complete, polished reveal
- Focus entirely on the work without managing audience expectations

If you're working on something particularly innovative or exploring a direction that might be hard to explain in fragments, private creation often makes more sense. It gives you the space to experiment freely without feeling like every iteration needs to be justified.

Many successful creators opt for a hybrid approach: developing the foundation in private until they're confident in the direction, then sharing selected aspects of the process once the core vision is solidified. This gives you both creative freedom and the benefits of audience engagement.

Choose the approach that aligns with your comfort level and the nature of your project. There's no single right answer—just what works best for your specific situation and creative temperament.

Tracking Progress

When working on longer projects, it's easy to lose sight of how far you've come or feel like you're not making sufficient progress. Keep a simple creative dashboard that tracks:

- Key milestones achieved (to remind yourself of wins along the way)
- Current focus areas (to maintain clarity on priorities)
- Open questions or challenges (to identify where you might need help)
- Next actions (to always know your immediate next step)
- Target completion dates (to maintain momentum)

This bird's-eye view of your project helps prevent getting lost in the details or feeling overwhelmed. It also provides motivation as you see your progress accumulate over time. Even on days when you feel stuck, being able to look back at how far you've come can renew your enthusiasm.

A simple note in your preferred tool (Notion, Google Docs, even a physical notebook) is all you need. The act of regularly updating this dashboard also creates a natural moment to reflect on your progress and realign with your vision if needed.

Integration Strategies

Creating content with AI is just the beginning. The real value comes from integrating that content into your broader creative ecosystem and workflow.

Building a Content Engine

Instead of viewing your creations as isolated pieces, think in terms of building a content engine—a systematic approach that consistently generates material for multiple platforms and purposes.

Start by creating cornerstone content—substantial, high-value material like guides, videos, or courses that represent your best work. Then use AI to help you extend the value of this investment:

1. **Extract**: Identify key ideas, quotes, and insights from your cornerstone content
2. **Transform**: Convert these elements into different formats (text to image, long-form to short-form)
3. **Distribute**: Adapt the content for different platforms while maintaining a consistent message
4. **Connect**: Create pathways that lead audiences from bite-sized content back to your cornerstone material

This approach maximizes the impact of your creative work while maintaining coherence across your entire content ecosystem. It's especially valuable when you're stretched thin or need to maintain a consistent presence across multiple channels.

The content engine model moves you from reactive, one-off creation (which can be exhausting) to strategic,

systematic production that builds on itself over time.#
BE THE CEO OF YOUR OWN IMAGINATION

YOU GOT THIS!